The Autism Sisterhood

A (Brief) Manual

Michele C. Brooke

Preface

This book began as a thought: What if one of my good friends learned her child had autism? What would I say? How would I use my experience to help her navigate this new road? Thus, began my project of writing down words of encouragement and support and, *best of all*, real-life ideas and suggestions to help guide her [you] through this new journey.

Between you and me, I am very thankful for what life has brought my way because it has made all the difference. I have two boys diagnosed with high functioning autism. When my oldest son was first diagnosed, I had no idea what autism really was. This, of course, is no longer the case.

The Autism Sisterhood: A (Brief) Manual is designed to be a starting point. It's short because I know you don't have much free time to sit without interruption, and it's small because I hope that once you've read it, you'll place it in your purse or backpack and pass it along to another mom (or dad) who may need it.

We're all in this together—learning, supporting, and laughing. So, should your son or daughter receive an autism diagnosis, please take a moment. Deep inhale. Slow exhale. Relax and know that autism is an incredible journey, and you all are going to be just fine.

The Autism Sisterhood

Hello and welcome to *The Autism Sisterhood*. What? You've never heard of such a group? Let me tell you a little bit about it. It's only for the brave, the creative, and the determined. However, please don't check your sense of humor at the door because that's a big part of the sisterhood too!

Most likely you arrived here by different paths. Perhaps autism took you by surprise, or it was something you suspected, researched, thought about. Whatever your path, this is an amazing journey. Think of it as a kayaking trip down a radiant river. At times, quiet and slow. Other moments are swift and rapid, taking your breath away. And, yes, sometimes you'll simply flip over and fall face first into the water!

But, that' okay, because that's why we're here...to reach out a dry hand and help you back into the kayak, back on your journey.

This sisterhood is unlike any other. Members come from unexpected places, and once here, they're bonded.

Why? Because they understand; they hope; they guess; they listen.

Who's in the sisterhood? Moms, sisters, friends, family, often they are a person who has a child with special needs or are close to someone who has autism. Even guys are welcomed in the sisterhood. We invite one and all! After all, we're all in this sisterhood for one purpose: to help these beautiful children navigate their world.

The members of your sisterhood are some of your best resources and often come with tried and tested ideas and suggestions. A lot of what I have learned along my journey has been from these very people and some I have learned on my own.

The Autism Sisterhood is a compilation of ideas and suggestions which I have collected and want to share with you. They are tidbits that have help to keep my family afloat and thriving. They are ideas I would share with you if we knew each other from long ago and found ourselves in the same boat (or kayak) once again.

Welcome aboard.

Nudge Your Way In

Some of the most wonderful members of the sisterhood have been therapists that we have met, particularly speech and occupational therapists. These professionals tend to have an amazing depth of compassion and knowledge. Enlist them into your circle. Watch their sessions with your child, bring a notebook and take notes, ask questions, find out what you can do at home to reinforce what they are already doing. Ask your therapists for "homework assignments" to reinforce therapy sessions at home, as well as request web sites or manufacturers that specialize in special needs items. Then, turn your home into an extension of their office.

The truth is that speech and occupational therapy sessions are indeed wonderful. However, they only last for 30-45 minutes per week—twice a week if you're lucky. Your child needs more.

Research. Research. Research. Yes, during all of that spare time you have, search for different tools you can bring into your home to facilitate speech and occupational therapy and then talk about your findings with your therapist. Bounce ideas off of her or him.

This brings me to one of my favorite topics: special needs catalogs. Oh, these are fun to browse. An invaluable collection of ideas, special needs catalogs are wonderful resources. Locate the catalogs by searching the Internet or asking for recommendations from therapists.

Some of my favorites include:

1) Southpaw Enterprises, Inc. www.southpawenterprises.com (I'm always in favor of going online; however, it really is worth it to order the catalog so you can spend time browsing each page.)

2) School Specialty's Abilitations Catalog www.schoolspecialty.net (So many great tools. Again, order the catalog)

3) Super Duper Publications www.superduperinc.com (Give me the latest Super Duper catalog, a hot cup of coffee and some page markers, and I'm set for some serious shopping. Their products are innovative and well made.)

4) LinguiSystems, Inc. www.linguisystems.com (Be sure to check out their Autism & PDD software programs. "Buddy Bear"—one of the program's main characters—is sure to become a household name in your family. Note: even if your child isn't computer savvy yet, you can use the mouse for them.)

Sisterhood Tip: as an eco-friendly move on your part, please pass along the catalog to other sisterhood moms or special needs teachers when you're finished.

Singing Songs

Music is huge. I have found music to be an incredible facilitator of speech and learning, and best of all, when the music is playing you don't have to be. I'm always on the lookout for ways I can continue to help my kids while I'm doing something else, be it driving, cooking or simply needing a few minutes to unwind.

This is where music comes in. However, not any singer, song or rhythm will do. You want to look for quality and purpose. My favorite music genre are speech songs (I just made this genre up. I'm not sure if it really exists, but it should—*Merriam Webster take note*)—albums created to help encourage talking and conversations.

Where do you find these types of albums? Again turn to the Internet and those special needs catalogs. There are all kinds of songs, some even focus on the beat of the music and slow it down to encourage calming. Now, what could be better?

Musicians and albums we enjoy include:

Genevieve Jereb's *Cool Bananas* and *Jumpin' Jellybeans* come with us on long car trips (Note: you will likely find yourself singing along—her songs are catchy and fun) (www.sensorytools.net)

Cathy Bollinger's *My Turn, Your Turn—Songs for Building Social Skills* is great, as is, *Singing Words—Songs for Language Development.* (www.rivannamusic.com)

Kiss Your Brain! and *Is Everybody Happy?* by Dr. Jean Feldman (www.drjean.org)

Kids' Express~Conversation Station by Rachel Arntson and Chez Raginiak (Writers and Developers) and Bill Scherer, Robin Medrud (Vocals and Narrators) Ania and Minika Raginiak (www.expresstrain.org)

Sisterhood Tip: Begin your audio collection with up-beat albums to play in the morning, calming playlists when your child is over stimulated or upset, teaching albums during the afternoon and albums that encourage sleep in the evening.

Expand and Elaborate

My oldest son was a huge fan of <u>Goodnight Moon</u> by Margaret Wise Brown. Wanting to encourage this literary love, I found everything I could that was related to <u>Goodnight Moon</u>. We had the big board book, the little board book, the audio book, the video, story props and even the game. It was a great way of illustrating how the same story could be expressed in various ways. He was learning vocabulary, reading comprehension, and creativity.

And, here's a secret: the best part of <u>Goodnight Moon</u> was relating it to everyday items; it was like going on a treasure hunt. For example, we would go through the book, reading the sentences, and then we would find the same object in our house. Showing him a real sock or a real clock would follow reading "Goodnight clocks, goodnight socks". *Fortunately,* for "goodnight mouse," we used a stuffed animal!

The key is discovering something your child likes and then broadening its teaching scope. Get creative; this can really be fun!

Sisterhood Tip: Enlist the help of your speech therapist and ask for a listing of good books and then find real objects that you can relate to the story. Another example, for the book <u>Brown Bear, Brown Bear, What Do You See?</u> By Eric Carle, you can use little figurines to represent each animal.

Indoor picnic

Speaking of using books as tools to explore the world, food books are a lot of fun and can be a creative way to introduce new foods to your child. Case in point: The Very Hungry Caterpillar by Eric Carle makes a delightful theme for an indoor picnic. If you have a picky eater, remember they don't *have* to eat the food. They can simply explore the different textures, shapes, sizes and smells.

Invite your friends and their children over for some cuisine observations. Throw out a blanket and have everyone sit (or wiggle or stand or whatever works), and then bring out the book. As you read through the various foods that the caterpillar munches on, introduce the actual item to the children. Let them explore it, touch it, mush it, whatever they'd like.

Introduce it as whole, then slice it and let them smell it, lick it, taste it. It's a fun way to explore new foods without having the pressure of them *having* to eat it.

Sisterhood Tip: Fruits that are a lot of fun include pineapples (so hard and bumpy on the outside, sweet and bright on the inside) and kiwi (they have a fun, green color with pretty little black seeds). I like foods that look one way on the outside, yet are so different inside.

Out on the Farm

This is one of our latest entertaining activities. Yes, you may think that I need to get out more, but, hey, in the sisterhood this is entertainment and when it works, it's literally awesome.

In childhood it seems farm animals are everywhere. They're cute; they make distinct noises and typically land the lead roles in cartoons. More than likely, your child has been exposed to them multiple times. Take it one step further and take your little guys on a farm animal scavenger hunt.

When we need a break from the house or are unwinding from a day of school, we drive to the country. We have a relaxing 20-minute car route where I talk about everything I see. It's quite the monologue.

We drive over canals, past barns and fields. In addition to identifying objects and commenting on the sky, I also slow down or stop and point out grazing cattle or horses so they can see the real life version of what they read about in books or see on television.

The key is commenting on *everything*. Here's why: I remember one of my friends telling me that her three-year old always asked so many questions. The mom was relieved whenever she had a break from the constant inquiries. I did not have that issue. However, that got me thinking: kids ask questions to socialize, but also to learn. I wanted to make sure my guys learned everything even if they didn't ask. So began my talking about everything—what I see, how I feel, what I think.

Sisterhood Tip: I have found that our kids absorb so much, even if they don't appear engaged in an activity; they are learning. The information is getting soaked up and comes out when you least expect it. These kids are sharp!

Celebrating Holidays

In the sisterhood, holidays are different. My advice: let go and follow the child's lead.

Here's what I've learned: Halloween is fun. Costumes are cool. Trick or treating is exciting. However, that's not necessarily true for everyone. Costumes may feel scratchy, and trick-or-treating may be confusing and loud.

My advice is don't get caught it up what "you should do or wear." Let your child wear what they find comfortable and go to the local carnival anyway. They'll have more fun, and that's what it's about.

Sisterhood Tip: search for easy-to-wear costumes that fit more like typical clothes. Have your child dress up a few times for practice before the big night. When the big night comes and they totally ignore all of your preparation and forethought and refuse to wear the costume, well, ditch the costume and go anyway. It'll make for a good story to tell your sisterhood. *They'll understand.*

The same goes for visiting pumpkin patches, photos with Santa and opening presents. Our kids may not think the idea is as great as we do, and that's okay. Remember, a lot of the traditions surrounding holidays are for the child's enjoyment; it's their time!

Case in point: On our second annual visit to the pumpkin patch, my son was enamored with the ladies selling the pumpkins. They were older and had gray hair just like his speech therapist whom he adored. All he wanted to do was to go and sit beside them and smile. Forget the pumpkins. Forget cute pumpkin patch pictures. He just wanted to sit beside the ladies. So that's what he did. *Carpe Diem.*

Who's teaching whom?

One of the great secrets of this sisterhood is the day-to-day journey. The immense joy found in getting eye contact, following directions, receiving verbal requests or even being lied to. Yes, I got excited the first time my son lied to me! It was a simple lie. I don't even recall what it involved. However, it showed that he got the concept that what he says can have a social impact.

It was huge. I called my mom. I bragged to my husband, his speech therapist and his teachers. My son lied, and I was so excited! He *got it*. And it's those little "got it" moments that are so joyous.

The way I see it, children on the spectrum are teachers. They teach us to slow down. They teach us to focus on the little things and remind us that the little things aren't so little after all. Sometimes developmental milestones take many, many steps to reach. However, when they get there (and they will), it's so exciting.

Sisterhood Tip: Find someone you can share these moments with. Don't ever think they're too trivial. They're amazing!

Shopping 101

Okay, here's the deal with most children on the autism spectrum. They're not likely to ask you for anything. Materialism is not in their nature. I'm always amazed at how I can go down the toy aisle in stores and neither of my boys ever exclaims, "I want that." Of course, if they were to do that, I would instantly buy it. *Disclaimer: Dear sons, once you're at the stage in life when you discover that mom would buy you anything you want, this rule may change, especially if the request involves items with wheels that go really fast.*

Anyway, the thing is these kids *like* toys, and they would like to play with them. However, they're not as likely to point this fact out to you, as would most children.

What to do? One solution I found was to listen to other kids comment and talk about what they like. One of my good friends has a son the same age as mine who told me that he wanted to be an astronaut when he grew up. He liked astronauts and space—*I wonder if my son would to?*

So, I began an intensive search on the Internet for space toys, puzzles, stickers, coloring books, etc. And, you know what? He did like space and can now identify planets, comets, space shuttles and astronauts. We both had fun exploring something new.

Sisterhood Tip: Introduce different toys to your child. The same thing goes for movies. I like to know which ones are popular with the preschool and kindergarten crowd and see if my guys like them too.

Who knew?

Since we're already discussing toys, here's another lesson for the sisterhood: toys aren't always found in the toy aisle or decked out in colorful packaging. Remember, kids on the autism spectrum are cool. They're interested in examining the details in what you may call "ordinary stuff." In other words, what they want to play with may be different than what's advertised on cable.

For example: At one time, my son loved plastic bananas. The kind you find in the floral department. They're realistic; they're made for arrangements; they were the most awesome thing he had ever seen! Many times I was able to complete a full round of grocery shopping just by letting him play with the plastic banana.

For Christmas that year my sister bought him twenty plastic bananas and wrapped them in a big box. It was the best present ever. What's better than one banana, but twenty bananas? He loved it.

Whatever "toy" your child is interested in, use it to help facilitate interaction or just plain fun. Play hide-n-seek with the banana; have the banana talk about the weather; have the banana ask for something to drink, and, most importantly, keep an extra banana in your purse for those moments when your child needs something that makes them happy.

Sisterhood Tip: Get creative. Perhaps, your child likes toothbrushes, yep, I said toothbrushes. Head to the dental aisle and start a collection of the most unusual toothbrushes you can find. You might be surprised at the variety. Once established, you and your child can observe the different textures, shapes, sizes, colors and even sounds.

Hugging Trees

Playing outdoors is one of our favorite things to do. It's under the sun, and I teach my sons about planting seeds, watering flowers, and identifying whether the clouds are white or gray. I've also learned to turn our backyard into a sensory garden.

For sounds, not only is there the dancing of the leaves, but also the ping of metal wind chimes and the hollow clunk of bamboo wind chimes. Next, I employ the sense of smell with an herb garden. I talk about the herbs; we pick them and then take in their scents. Ok, sometimes it's just me smelling the herbs, but hey, it's relaxing and I enjoy it!

I also grow veggies in the summer and have my sons "harvest" them for dinner. They're not into eating all of them, but they do pick them, bring them inside, and watch as I wash and cook them.

Sisterhood Tip: Other favorite outdoor activities include bubble machines, sand boxes, dirt and rocks. It's all simple, and yet, it's also very sensory-oriented.

The Explore Basket

This idea came to me as my son and I were standing in an arts and craft store. He was mesmerized by all of the holiday decorations. They were everywhere. He stood, looked, jumped up and down, and *explored*. There were so many sights, sounds, colors, etc. We stayed quite a while and were asked several times if we could be helped. Each time I replied, "We're just looking." And, that's exactly what we did. We looked. We learned.

As I stood there, I came to realize that holidays are a sensory blitz with lights, sounds, smells, songs, characters and traditions coming at you from every direction. There is so much that it can be hard to soak it all in, especially at holiday parties when it's combined with the excitement and noise of lots of people.

Hence, the Explore Basket idea was born. I made it for my sons' class and each season/holiday I changed it out. The first basket (it's just a large wicker basket) was "Explore Autumn," in which I brought together a collection of colored leaves, small hay bale, pumpkins, gourds, a pilgrim's hat, and scarecrow. Basically, I went to different stores looking for items the kids might see at someone's house or classroom. I got items they would most likely recognized (jack-o-lanterns), as well as some new ones (like cornucopia)—always looking for ways to build vocabulary.

The beauty of the Explore Basket is that it's all hands-on. The kids can touch the scarecrow; they can pull out the stuffing if they want. There is no "don't touch that" rule—it's all about learning. The key to the basket is variety, textures and scents.

The scent part of the basket is a lot of fun. How often does a certain smell bring back a memory of an event or location for you? That's why, for Christmas, the basket is filled with candy canes and cinnamon sticks.

Another fun (and helpful) theme is birthday parties. For this topic, the basket is piled high with wrapped gifts (for the kids to practice giving to one another), party hats, party whistles/toys. This way the kids are introduced to all of the items that they would typically see at a party and have the opportunity to investigate them in a calmer environment. The Explore Basket provides kids with a path to evaluate and understand some of the nuances of a holiday or event without it being too overwhelming.

Sisterhood Tip: Talk with the other moms and dads in the classroom to see what events are unsettling for their kids and see if you can find ways to create a basket to help them work through it.

Learning to Read

A powerful lesson that my little guys have taught me is that they are learning all the time, and the more I capitalize on that fact, the more life becomes a little clearer for them. I want to introduce them to all kinds of new concepts, vocabulary *and* communication outlets, like reading and writing (or typing).

Keeping the fun factor high, we do all kinds of things with words. When we go to the beach, I use a stick and write in the sand: "I like __." I change up the words; I make it silly. The guys love it, and the awesome part is when they start joining in and coming up with their own ideas.

You can make words using modeling clay, finger paint, white erase boards, letter stamps and more.

Other helpful reading aides are read-along books. Some of my favorite read along-style books are found in a series published by Candlewick Press. The series is called *Read, Listen & Wonder* and each book includes a read-along CD and teaches children about different animals like barn owls, blue whales and giant octopuses. So, now they're learning to read, expanding their vocabulary and possibly sparking new interests.

Our favorites:

<u>Big Blue Whale with Audio: Read, Listen & Wonder</u> by Nicola Davies

<u>White Owl, Barn Owl with Audio: Read, Listen & Wonder</u> by Nicola Davies

Sisterhood Tip: Don't think that you have to save read along books for long car trips. Most children audio books are fairly short. You'll be surprised how many renditions you can get in on the way to school and back. Also, be sure to check out downloadable audio books—you can buy the corresponding book at the bookstore so your child can follow along.

While we're on the topic of reading, I'd like to share with you a company that publishes wonderful books that are known as "social stories." Social stories essentially help kids understand how to act or react to a certain situation. They help the world make sense.

Natural Learning Concepts (www.nlconcepts. com) publishes social stories, along with other helpful products. One series is titled "Now I Get It! ~Social Stories that build confidence and demonstrate appropriate behavior." Examples of subjects include "Answering Questions," "Saying 'Hi' and 'Bye,'" and "Playing with a Friend."

Play it Again

These kids are typically excellent at focusing on videos and absorbing the information. I say make the most of on this trait by finding videos that teach social skills, reading, math, telling time, counting money, etc.

Again, look through special need catalogs to find titles. Then read the reviews. Reviews can provide good insight into the video, as well as suggest other titles that may be useful. Amazon is my favorite web site for reading DVD reviews.

Following are a handful of videos that we have used and really liked.

Action Words! Series by Baby Bumblebee (www.babybumblebee.com)

Olivia & Otis by Baby Bumblebee

Baby Babble by Talking Child (www.talkingchild.com)

Bounce DVD Series by Spectrum Connections (www.spectrumconnections.com)

Kibbles Rockin' Clubhouse Vol. 1 Expressing Yourself by NoteAbilities Inc. (www.noteabilities.com)

Meet the Sight Words Series by Preschool Prep Company (www.preschoolprepco.com)

I Can Read Songs for Reading by LaDonna Wicklund (www.icanreadsongs.org)

Let's Play Volume 2 Classic Series by Watch Me Learn (www.watchmelearn.com)

Sisterhood Tip: Titles are being added all the time. Search the Internet, read reviews and see which ones are a good fit for you and your child. Ask other moms in your sisterhood about DVDs that captivate their child. Videos can be a great teaching tool.

Experimenting with Science

You never know what will inspire your child down an adventurous and intriguing new learning path. Introduce your child to science. It can be fascinating for both of you!

Explore colors: mix food coloring with water and then blend the colors to make new colors. Let the kids guess the color the two will make (if they are non-verbal, have some markers on the table and have them touch the matching color).

Talk about liquids and solids. Yes, talk to your three and four-year olds about liquids and solids. It can be fun. Use visual aids like Jello, ice cubes, etc. Talk about how some items can be liquid and then change into a solid and vice versa. Let them help you observe how the popsicle they are holding is a solid and can melt into a liquid. This experiment is exceptionally fun on a hot summer afternoon.

Find a big handheld magnifying glass and go on a safari around the house or backyard. Have your child look at some of his or her favorite food or toys up close. Talk about everything you see. Compare bigger and smaller. Talk about what you see that was unexpected.

Explore animal habitats with an ant farm, or teach the life cycle of a butterfly with a butterfly kit that can be purchased online or from a store. It's a great feeling when your child discovers a new interest. Take it and run with it.

For example, if he or she is captivated by the ant farm, then use that as a communication tool. Ask, "Where do you think this ant is going?" "Is the ant big or small?" "Is it living or nonliving?" If your child is nonverbal or doesn't answer questions yet, provide the answers for them. Find books about animal habitats and read them aloud. Get a large sheet of paper and a thin black marker and have your child make "ant tracks." Have them follow instructions: "make four ant tracks," "make really messy ant tracks," or "make really neat ant tracks." Change it up. The key is to target something they like and use it in other ways to engage and teach them.

Sisterhood Tip: My thinking is that the more your child understands his or her world, the less confusing or scary it might be for them. Search the Internet and teacher supply stores for early science experiments for preschoolers and kindergarteners. There are all kinds of fun, easy activities. Many, in fact, you may recall doing as a kid.

Little Chefs

Help your children learn how individual pieces come together to make a whole.

Time to get out the mixing bowl, spoons and their favorite cake or brownie mix. My guys love to cook. I measure, and they pour and stir. They learn about different ingredients, waiting, turn taking, following directions, and of course, cooking.

Top the cake or brownies with chocolate chips and have your child put them on one at a time. Create a chocolate chip pattern or ask them to place a particular number of chips in one section. Use your imagination and watch their imagination grow!

When cooking with your little chefs, it's a good idea to have a backup plan. For example, if he or she wants to make a peanut butter and jelly sandwich and while spreading the ingredients, the bread crumbles, tears or essential becomes unappetizing, have something else on hand that they can eat, or simply have a "practice session" when no one is really, really hungry.

Sisterhood Tip: Remember to always explain everything you're doing. When they're pouring say, "pour,

pour, pour into the bowl." If they really took to the science lessons about solids and liquids, you can ask them questions like, "Is the flour a solid or liquid?" Adapt your conversation to match their interests.

Embrace Electronics

Talk about attention getting! My guys gravitate toward electronic gizmos, and, like videos, you can use them to teach.

Handheld game consoles that use stylus pens are a hit at my house—I like them because they work on fine motor skills and encourage problem solving (think: puzzles) as well as creativity, reading, and math; my boys like them because they're fun!

We also use several iTunes apps. Visit Apple's iTunes web site (www.apple.com/itunes) and enter the keyword "autism" in the search box. You will discover all kinds of apps that are geared toward teaching kids everything from vocabulary to recognizing emotions. Best of all, you can upload them to your iPhone or iTouch and carry them with you. Stuck in the check out line? No problem, introduce the app to your child and enjoy the peace. Everyone is content.

I New electric gadgets hit the market every day. One of my favorite finds is the *Tag Reading System* by LeapFrog (www.leapfrog.com) and I like it for three reasons: 1) It's engaging and encourages reading, word recognition, reading comprehension, 2) The Tag "pen" is held in the hand like a pencil (OK, not really a pencil because the Tag pen is much wider, but it works on fine motor skills), and 3) It uses real books. I am a big proponent of electronics and their usefulness in helping teach our children; however, I also like the old-fashioned feel of a book!

Grab Some Popcorn and Sit

There are two movies I would recommend to parents who are just entering the autism sisterhood. The first, *A Mother's Courage: Talking Back to Autism* a documentary by Fridrik Thor Fridriksson (www.amotherscourage.org), gives me goose bumps just thinking about it. If you ever question whether or not these kids are absorbing information, then this documentary will erase all doubt. This movie gives you insight, perspective, and hope. These kids are smart!

The second movie would be HBO Films' *Temple Grandin* (www.hbo.com/movies/temple-grandin), which is based on the life of a truly amazing woman. *Temple Grandin* will further validate the fact that autism is an incredible journey. The movie helps you view the world from a different perspective. It gives you a glimpse into how someone with autism processes information. It's both enlightening and inspiring.

I always like movies with good endings.

Building Big People

As a parent, perhaps one of the great gifts you can give your child is self-esteem. It's something that will last a lifetime and helps you all get through each day.

Accentuate the positive. When you've asked your child to do something, and they do it—that's *awesome*! Say, "Great listening!" or "Good following directions!" When they transition well to a change in schedule, no matter how small, brag to them. Saying, "Great job being flexible!" helps to teach them what being flexible means and shows them that they *can* do it.

When I catch my boys doing something impressive, I compliment them right away. I also like to revisit the situation later that same day by talking about how proud I was that they did something a certain way. You can even create a "flexibility chart" or "great behavior chart" and have them place a sticker on the chart every time they demonstrate a wonderful behavior.

I also believe in affirmations. We have a little bedtime tradition that we've been doing since the boys were very little. Each night before they go to sleep, I tell my boys that they are smart; they are kind; they are strong. It's something I believe and that I want them to believe too.

Pay Attention to Yourself

Now, I am all for treating yourself to a spa day or some down time; however, what I'm talking about here is paying attention to how you *feel* when you're sick, mad, frustrated, anxious etc.

Imagine if you are not able to tell someone that you're in a bad mood and simply don't want to participate in an activity, or perhaps, you're frustrated with a project and cannot verbally express your feelings. By understanding how you feel at different times, you're better able to step into your child's shoes.

Autism often requires you to be a detective. With enough information, most actions make sense!

Whenever I have gotten laryngitis, I am reminded of how much I use my words to communicate. It would be a tough world to navigate if I could not speak or understand words. *Remember that feeling.* Being empathetic is an essential factor in your child's success.

Talking

Talking is huge. Your talking that is. In the beginning of your journey, your child may not communicate much, so it's up to you to tell them about the world. Ask questions. Answer your own questions. Discuss the weather, food, books, everything.

Keep it simple, but keep talking. "Oh look, the sky is blue. I like the sky. It makes me happy."

Verbalize your feelings. When you're happy say, "I'm smiling because I'm happy" or "I like eating ice cream. That makes me happy."

Teach your child about the importance of pointing at items. Say, "Look I am *pointing* at the truck." While walking, talk about different items you pass or step over. At the park talk about what other people are doing: "Oh look, that lady is walking a dog" or "Wow, look how high that girl is swinging."

When you bend down to pick something up, talk about it. "I am bending down to pick up this book." When you brush your teeth, talk about it. "I am brushing my teeth to keep them clean."

The more you talk, the more your child absorbs language and vocabulary. The more you talk, the more the world makes sense to them.

Building the Sisterhood

I love the sisterhood! It's always growing and expanding with each new person I meet. What I appreciate about it the most is that it does not require daily conversations or frequent visits. Who has the time?

The sisterhood is there for you. It's that friend you can call up and share good news with, like when your child says "bye" to their teacher for the first time or answers a "yes or no" question. Those moments are huge, and the sisterhood *gets it*.

I would encourage you to share information with other parents, teachers or therapists. If I come across a new toy or video that really sparks an interest in my boys, I send out a quick email. You never know what will help make life clearer for your child or someone else's. And, when you find that cool teaching toy or communication venue, that is an awesome feeling. Share what you learn!

Inviting teachers into your sisterhood is important. After all, they are the ones interacting with your child for hours each day. I like to brainstorm with my sons' teachers to come up with new ideas and to reinforce what they are learning at school. I also have a little habit of telling the teacher and aides "thank you" at the end of each day. Not only are my sons' teachers good educators, but they also have a huge heart. Their job requires a ton of energy, patience, and commitment. What impresses me most, perhaps, is their love and respect for each child. So, if this describes your child's teacher, remember to tell them "thank you."

The Big Picture

There's a big picture to autism that you *have* to see.

How you view your child's behavior has a direct impact on both of you. It's important to not view your child's behavior as a negative reaction toward you. The fact is not you or anyone else is "being ignored" or that the child "is busy" or in their "own little world." It's much, much more.

You have to try and see the world from their viewpoint. You have to understand that they may hear, see, taste and smell differently than others and are reacting accordingly. Finally, you have to be a scientist—guessing, researching, and trying new ideas, new paths to make your child's journey easier.

Our paths will be varied. Our accomplishments will be great. The sisterhood is about embracing autism and its road. It's about traveling and overcoming. You set your sights on the ground in front of you and roll with the curves and bends. The sisterhood is proactive, creative, hardworking, and determined. This sisterhood is also compassionate towards each other and towards these wonderful children who are sharing this journey with us.

Enjoy. Laugh. Work hard. And have a cup coffee (or two).